Psychedelic Logic

Shifts in the Perception of Reality

by

Barry F. Satchel

Dorrance Publishing Co
585 Alpha Drive
Pittsburgh, PA 15238
Visit our website at www.dorrancebookstore.com

ISBN: 979-8-88729-105-5
eISBN: 979-8-88729-605-0

Prologue

If you live long enough, you'll reach a time in which you have more sunsets behind you than you have sunrises in front of you. Right around this phase, your outlook on life changes and you start to value things a little differently. You prioritize quality over quantity—facts over fiction—and time becomes your most valuable possession. You start to believe your "lying eyes" over the talking heads on radio and TV, and you realize you've been lied to your entire life. All in an effort to keep you distracted, appeased, or suppressed. You start to accept life "as you've known it," or at least thought you knew it, was all a lie and the answer to "Are we alone?" has already been asked and answered. Mankind is at the infancy stage of understanding the universe and all it has to offer. You'll eventually come to the conclusion that the protection the powers that be were providing was not for you but for them, as they used every available platform to keep you in the cold, dark hallows of ignorance. Welcome to the light.

Foreword

This was not written to answer all or any of the questions of the universe but to merely start you on the process of objectively thinking and questioning the irrational. I am not offering you a fish, I'm offering to teach you how to fish. Just as I'm sure there is a cure for cancer, but there is more money in the treatment than the cure. It's not the front-page headlining event or breaking news that every channel is focused on; it's the story they are not telling you that's doing all the damage which you need to know about. When the powers that be can't contain a story, they merely create a larger event to distract your focus. Follow the money and the power and you'll find the answers of which you seek. Be quick to listen, slow to speak, and slow to react, and only then will you be able to discern the facts.

If you've read my previous writings you are probably aware of my background and ethos. The events that shaped my thought processes leads me to these conclusions, rather they be real or perceived, some, if not all, are at least viable possibilities. First and foremost, I have no evidence that any of the manifestations you are about to read are true or even happened the way I'm suggesting. However, with that being said, "If it walks like a duck, and quacks like a duck, then it's probably a duck." As far back as I've researched leadership and governments, they have been dishonest with their citizens under the guises attempting to protect them. However, governments tend to be self-serving, especially in republics and democracies where officials are elected by their peers. You see, once you've been elected, your job is not to serve your constituents but to oblige the special interest contributors who donated the most to your campaign for the possibility of reelection. If your sponsor's interests are not addressed, your next campaign will not be a success. Conversely, in autocratic-controlled societies, they don't sugarcoat the rule of law. The people can either accept it, be imprisoned, or die fighting for their voices to be heard.

It has been said before, and I believe it to be true, that power corrupts. The moment a régime or its representatives are not held accountable is the precise instant that liberties and the inalienable rights of the people to be informed are lost.

The foundational rules of criminology are question everything, take nothing for granted, and the most obvious is sometimes the least likely to be the answer. What if history was not history but his-story and not a true depiction of the past, but a reiterating of the first lie told and repeated through time? What if the Roswell UFO incident actually occurred? What if several significant events of the past decades were not of chance but part of a larger series of staggered staged events implemented to distract society from the greatest heist the world has never seen and yet still goes unrecognized? What if this thievery involved the reallocation of more than twenty-two trillion dollars, supposedly "elected" officials, and the Federal Reserve, culminating in the largest transfer of wealth from the poor and middle classes to the rich and wealthy in the world's most powerful nation?

Have you ever wondered why in 2008 the worst-case scenario became a reality reckoning? Some people lost everything up to and including their lives, committing suicide, overwhelmed by the gravity of their financial situation, and no one was held accountable for the debacle? During a time when uncertainty was the only certainty, with banks closing like windows before a sandstorm, the heads of the most powerful financial institutions in the country were relieved from command. Multi-million-dollar payouts and exit bonuses were being paid out as rewards for their failures in leadership. Now synonymous with the phrase "too big to fail," the very institutions responsible for the economic collapse were charged with fixing the economy and given amnesty for their previous transgressions. By some estimates, the richest 1 percent of the country controls an estimated 50 percent of the country's wealth, and the bottom 90 percent owes 73 percent of the debt. While other estimates insist that if pensions and social security are excluded, the richest 1 percent of the American population owns 34.6 percent of the country's total wealth, and the next 19 percent owns 50.5 percent. Thus, the top 20 percent of Americans owns 85 percent of the country's wealth, and the bottom 80 percent of the population owns 15 percent.

One might ask; "What would the top 1 percent want with the rest of the wealth?" *Audentes Fortuna Juvat* (Latin for "fortune favors the bold").

The 1 percent didn't get to be rich by waiting for opportunities; they created them. How much is too much when there is never enough? What if, as a collective society, we were all being hoodwinked...and they are all in on it? What if a host of seemingly random events, plotted through time, was actually orchestrated to lull society into compliance, all in preparation for the coup de grace, ***too big to fail***?

Governments engage with their citizens in three ways: appeasements, distractions, or suppressions. Appeasements are concessions designed to quell hostilities and keep the natives at bay. Events such as elections, public assistance programs, stimulus programs, tax breaks, and tax refunds lull the public into believing someone cares, things can be made fair, and their voice is being heard. Distractions, the most popular of the choices, are presented in the forms of offensive military actions, racial tensions, social distancing, terroristic events or warnings, gun control, immigration, and national emergencies. Finally, the least popular but still very effective, is suppression.

Suppression is always used as a last resort. Events such as the Waco siege, the Ruby Ridge incident, and the Bundy standoff in Nevada, the 2019 COVID-19 world and national shutdowns make it appear as if the government is overstepping its authority. This tends to ignite the radicals along with disenfranchised, bringing an uncertainty to a very volatile situation.

What if the series of events including the First Gulf War in 1990, the 1993 attempt to bring the World Trade Center down, the 1995 bombing of the Alfred P. Murrah Building in Oklahoma City, the 1996 Khobar Towers bombing in Saudi Arabia, the October 2000 bombing of the *USS Cole* off the coast of Yemen, the Second Gulf War, the 9/11 World Trade Center tragedy/US Pentagon attack in 2001, subsequent invasions of Iraq and Afghanistan in 2002, the North Korean and Iranian nuclear programs crisis, the Malaysia Air Flight 370, COVID-19, the election of a reality TV star to the position of leader of the free world, and the seemingly out of nowhere resurgence of an old cold war enemy in Russia, and rise of China as a new Asian Pacific threat to US naval supremacy as a new world superpower were all parts of an ingenious, well-thought-out, seamlessly orchestrated, and patiently executed plan to distract the masses in the most complicated game of Three Card Monte ever devised?

The point is, there is always some exigent new crisis to worry about which distracts the public, and if that doesn't work, there's always the secondary game of "which cup is the red ball under" playing in the background concerning health care, unemployment, and immigration, being performed before our eyes. The objective is to keep you worried about events you can't control, thereby being distracted from what's really happening. As the old saying goes, just because I'm paranoid doesn't mean I'm not being followed, just as this may be crazy enough to be true.

If the greatest trick the Devil ever preformed was to make people believe he doesn't exist, then perhaps the greatest trick the 1 percenters can perform would be making the poor and middle class turn over their assets and feel good about doing so.

If you think about it just for a moment, never before in history has an individual with President Donald Trump's background and bio been successful in politics. A man who cheated on his first wife with his second wife, his second wife with his third, and his third wife with prostitutes, porn stars, and any random woman that would submit to his larger-than-life ego.

An individual that demands loyalty from any and every associate he interacts with, has none. Furthermore, this very same individual accused of sexual assault, financial impropriety, and failing to pay his acknowledged debts was still "elected" to the highest position in the land. I believe Trump's presidency was and is part of a larger well-thought-out and perfectly implemented plan to initiate a transfer of wealth never before seen, and this is precisely why his past indiscretions and obnoxious behavior is completely irrelevant. Although not outright mentioned, the US Federal Reserve not only set US economic policy, but by default world economic policy, as the US dollar is the world bench mark currency

In December of 1913 the Federal Reserve banking system was created to stabilize and centrally control the US monetary system. However, as many may not know, the Federal Reserve Banks are not part of the US federal government, but the twelve banks are independent private entities that act in concert with one another and the federal government to direct US monetary policies. Although the Fed Reserve was created by an act of Congress, nonetheless it is a private entity worth $4.5 trillion dollars.

This privacy allows the Fed Reserve to operate more like a business than a branch of government, freeing it from key congressional interferences. In December of 2008, the Fed Reserve balance sheets held nine hundred billion dollars of US debt. At the same time, the US as a nation was spiraling into one of the worst economic downturns and recessions experienced since the great depression of 1929 through 1939. So, the Fed Reserve made an agreement with the US federal government to start absorbing some of the debt in the form of mortgage-backed securities (six hundred billion dollars' worth) from what was considered the primary cause of the economic downturn, but as most things do not happen independently or in a vacuum, the automobile industry and the manufacturing industries were also throttling down as well. The Fed Reserve called their stabilization plan Quantitative Easing (QE), which would eventually swell their balance sheets to $4.5 trillion dollars of debt when it ended in 2014.

Since mortgage-backed securities (MBS) were the result of irresponsible lending practices and greed on behalf of banks and borrowers alike, the Fed Reserve did not feel obligated or responsible to bail the system out. However, if the nation is not making money, neither is the Fed Reserve, so the Fed Reserve had to "play ball," but if the Fed Reserve was going to play ball, it would be by their rules. The Fed Reserve desperately needed to shed the $3.6 trillion dollars of holdings it absorbed six years earlier, as it tried to prevent an unprecedented recession so it devised a plan to do so.

In June of 2018 the plan to return the Federal Reserve's balance sheets to what they considered to be a reasonably stable position, called Quantitative Tightening (QT), was initiated. Quantitative Tightening would encompass releasing fifty billion dollars a month of MBSs from the $3.6 trillion dollars of holdings they absorbed over the previous six years. However, for this plan to work, the conditions would have to be right, and parameters would need to be set. When the plan for QE was conceived, Barack Obama, a charismatic second-term president, was entering the "lame duck" phase of his final years as commander in chief and appeared to be readying a plan to turn over the reins to his then Secretary of State Hilary Clinton. Clinton, a not very well liked individual who had previously failed in a bid to be the first female president of the United States in 2008, as she then opposed Candidate Obama, had paid her dues and was now poised to take control.

Although it was Obama and Clinton's plan, it was not the Federal Reserve's nor the Republican Party's plan to allow the country to be continually managed by the Democrats. The Federal Reserve needed an individual that would implement their instructions without reservation and would not care about the political backlash from constituents and corporations. The play callers chose Donald J. Trump, a self-proclaimed self-made billionaire whose reality TV star status made him an instantly recognizable name and face, and while his business legend preceded him, his name itself was a brand. Trump's notoriety was just what the Federal Reserve needed to put their plan in action. Trump immediately went to work repeating his mantra of make America great again, providing the promise of change and distracting the masses as he went to work making America great again, or as some may say, pulling the Federal Reserve from the brink of insolvency.

In January of 2017, after the oath of office and swearing in, one of the Trump Administration's first acts was to begin the repeal of the Dodd Frank Act, thereby setting the conditions and preparing the economy for another housing market collapse. Fast forward one year, and at the beginning of 2018, interest rates for a thirty-year fixed Fannie Mae government-backed mortgage was 2.75 percent; by October of the same year, the rate was 5 percent. In real terms, this meant a four-hundred-thousand-dollars mortgage at 2.75 percent principal and interest (P&I) would be $1,633.00 a month; however, at a 5 percent interest rate, that same mortgage would be $2,147.00 (P&I), a $514.00 monthly increase. Remember back when the Federal Reserve initially agreed to start purchasing the mortgage based securities (MBS) in 2006? The Fed Reserve purchased them for two cents on the dollar. In 2018, when the Federal Reserve started reintroducing fifty billion dollars of securities and bonds back on the US stock market monthly, they were selling them for ninety cents on the dollar. Seemingly a good investment and wise financial move, the Federal Reserve had no choice but to repackage the MBS and reintroduce them to the investments and bonds markets as it was financially insolvent because of debt it took on in the form of MBS twelve years earlier. However, the long-term effects of these decisions are just coming to light.

For example, without a conversely increase in personal income, this increase in housing expenses will make housing unaffordable for many, thereby widening the wealth gap. By no means am I advocating any social justice to give everyone a house, but without affordable housing, big picture-wise, the nation's economic engine slows to a grinding and stops. Example, first quarter 2019 US economy starts to slow, and the Federal Reserve responds by freezing interest rates for two years (until first quarter 2021). This slowdown was a predictable result of Trump's trickledown economics tax plan, which gave the wealthy and large corporations huge, unprecedented tax cuts, believing they would reinvest the savings in the economy via jobs and increased production; however, they just retained the earnings and savings, and the economy continued to struggle. Equally, if housing is unavailable, rent will sky rocket as there are no options left except for multiple generations in one household or roommate cohabitation agreements, much like San Francisco, CA. To put it bluntly, I believe President Trump was put in office by the Federal Reserve to propel their financial agenda, getting a second crack of the wealth transfer whip. In late December 2019, rumblings of a virus spreading in a small Chinese city called Wuhan were slowly starting to make waves as it devoured the city; COVID-19 was officially here. In order for it to be a COVID-19, there had to be at least eighteen prior COVIDs as it was, and the virus was commensurate via a virus year, but COVID-19 would be different; it would be unflappable, unstoppable, and incurable. This retrovirus COVID-19 would be able to survive without a live host on multiple surfaces for a considerable time, transcend all boarders, and be easily communicable. COVID-19 would be a pandemic of biblical proportions so entrancing and polarizing, the wealth of most of the population could transferred to a select few, and no one would even notice. COVID-19 checked every box of governmental control. COVID-19 distracted, suppressed, and appeased the entire country and the world. As people were distracted with how deadly and communicable the disease was, suppressed by a government-ordered national shutdown of all nonessential organizations and finally appeased with federal stimulus checks as the US treasury issued out two trillion dollars in financial assistance to the crying masses, as the US Congress passed a 845-page stimulus package without really reading it. Originally said to have been originated in Wuhan, China, COVID-19 took over the world in a sweeping, merciless manor. Most people were carriers and spreaders before they ever knew it. With symptoms similar to the flu or a common cold, very few knew of the trouble that was brewing. COVID-19 was just what was needed to bring the world to its knees, not only as a pandemic and a distraction but also igniting a worldwide transfer of wealth, as if a meeting of the richest people in the world had occurred and a plan had been cultivated and enacted. Phase one would need to scare people into compliance; this would be accomplished by a complete shutdown of society, causing people to panic and hoard basic necessities. Phase two would be a full press media blitz with constant coverage spreading rumors of contamination sources, virus mutations, and ways of contacting the virus which has no cure and astronomical worldwide reports of deaths. Phase three would involve a slow reintegration of a new norm, with constant reminders of things are not the same, allowing business to re-open and people to venture out once again, as if operating at half capacity would somehow reduce the risk of being infected. People would be instructed to limit the size of crowds, limit the number of patrons in shops, stores, and restaurants, and submit liberties for the greater good of society. The final phase would be the new normal, with people focusing on their regained freedom and adjustments and not the transfer of wealth that had just occurred before their very eyes. No one would speak on the eleven trillion dollars collapsing the housing market overburdened by the record number of unemployed people unable to pay their mortgage, or the $275 billion automobile market collapsing as sales plummeted to a halt. No one would speak up of the hypocrisy of everyone touching money that had not been sanitized, or that patrons touched the carts at the grocery store or gas pumps. People didn't think about how everything in the grocery store had been possibly touched by someone infected with the virus, like a stocker or other customers, or that the same government that had redacted the Affordable Care Act now cared about the public's health care. No one spoke of employee's choice between going to work sick and getting a paycheck or staying home, starving, as a large portion of society lived paycheck to paycheck. However, the real crime was a majority of societies' wealth had just been transferred and picked right out of their pockets via stock market fluctuations, 401ks being looted, and home values plummeting. Donald Trump and the Federal Reserve had just solved their financial woes, and came out looking like heroes and smelling like roses. News of the coronavirus started to trickle out in late 2019. Simultaneously, President Donald Trump was facing an impeachment hearing in the US Senate. Needing a distraction from the impeachment and after years of trying to get China to renegotiate its less-than-balanced trade deal with the US, the coronavirus was just what the Trump Administration needed. With 1.4 billion people, China desperately needs international trade to keep its economy going and its people working and not disfranchised. Even if the coronavirus was all that it is what it was built up as, a few thousand Chinese dying from what is basically the flu does not register on anyone's radar unless a concerted effort is exorcised to highlight its prominence. In comes talk of a pandemic; out of nowhere, the 2019 coronavirus starts to spread like a bee pollenating flowers. As the world was unprepared for the ensuing plague, one by one, entire cities, followed by countries shut down to control the spread of the deadly virus. As countries started to shut down, so did their economies, followed by the world's economy, and as the virus spread, so did the rumors. Questions were being asked, but political officials had no answers, and the so-called experts were at a loss too, which allowed speculation to reign supreme. Everyone wondered why was COVID-19 so deadly when the previous COVID viruses didn't even registrar on the scale. How and why was the virus so deadly? Why did it spread so easily? And even after being infected and overcoming the disease, how could you be reinfected? Tens of thousands of people would die from it, and millions would be infected by it. Symptoms would be from mild to severe, and in some cases none at all. Worldwide focus on China being the origin of the coronavirus was killing demand for Chinese exports and driving down the world exchange markets, thereby effectively forcing China to reconsider its trade policies with the US and providing the US with more leverage at the trade table. Meanwhile, things were lining us for the Trump Administration to secure a trade deal, just before the national elections in November, as Trump was trying to get reelected for a second term and could benefit from a trade deal boost. Perhaps the coronavirus was created in a lab by some three letter US organization, i.e., CIA, NSA, FBI, CDC, or even perhaps MJ12, and taken to China to be release in an aerosol form on a subway or train and then just allowed to run its course so even if the virus was traced back to its origins, it would look like it originated in China? Even better when the Chinese denied creating such a menacing disease, the evidence would still point back to them. You may not know, no US department operates autonomously, but actually, they work in concert with one another towards the national interest. Furthermore, I find it strange that the very government that dismantled the Affordable Care Act and took away millions of Americans' health care suddenly became concerned about people's health. In my opinion, it's like your abuser beings concerned about the black eye they gave you. The government's ability to force people to have health care via the Affordable Care Act is no different that the government forcing people to have a retirement with the Social Security Act. These are the very same people whom dismantled the Dodd Frank Act from 2011 and then became concerned about the possible forty million families that were estimated to be homeless during the pandemic after the moratorium and mandate on rent and mortgage payments suspensions at the onset of the pandemic had expired. Prior to COVID-19, the Federal Reserve was basically insolvent because of its agreements with the US Government and absorbing debt for the previous six years and desperately needed a favorable business environment or a miracle to make this happen. The COVID-19 pandemic gave the US Federal Reserve backdoor access to the eleven-trillion-dollar housing market, setting us for another cents on the dollar fire sale and absorption. Primary mortgage insurance programs (PMIs) could not cover a housing collapse spread across the nation as the system was never designed for such a catastrophic event. If you recall, the Fed Reserve already held nine hundred billion dollars of US debt in the beginning of 2006 and agreed to take on another six hundred billion dollars in MBS, but that six hundred billion ended up being $3.6 trillion dollars, which makes their $4.486 trillion dollars of value a wash. Trump, being the Fed's man, is exactly why no political party initially affiliated themselves with him; he was not a Democrat, Republican, or an Independent, but was of no party affiliation.

It was only when he was a potential benefit to the Republican Party did they claim him, as the initial twenty Republican presidential candidates dropped out of the race one by one. If you recall, on election night 2016 every television station had Clinton winning by a landslide, then, all of a sudden, it was reported by Fox News that Trump had won. Just like that the narrative had changed; Trump came from behind out of nowhere to win the bid for the White House like a one-hundred-to-one race horse. The world was polarized, watching the most captivating reality TV show ever produced with a plot twist at the end that could only be described as epic, dejecting, and breathtaking, all in the same sentence. Perhaps it could be as simple as Trump was and is a Russian agent, propped up and cultivated over the years and activated as suggested in the book Collusion by Luke Harding. As hard as this may be to believe or swallow, if chapter eleven of the aforementioned book is true, there is no other plausible answer. Perhaps the easiest way to destroy America is from within, and what better way to do it than an elected official.

Again, I'm not saying that everything that happens is part of an orchestrated plan being controlled by a Grand Puppet Master; some damage is just collateral. However, I am implying things are not what they seem to be, and more often than not, the public is being controlled by the very media it seeks to keep them informed. This is precisely why President Trump has been unable to accomplish anything legislative outside of an Executive Order, as the DC insiders won't play with outsiders. Fast forward ten months to March of 2019, and as previously predicted, the economic conveyor belt starts to slow down. In March of 2019 the US Federal Reserve and the European Central Bank both abruptly changed course and froze interest rates for the rest of the year and predicted just one rate hike in 2021. These abrupt reverses in decision-making was a result of several factors, to include the trade wars the Trump Administration started with China, pulling out of the NAFTA with Mexico and Canada, and North Korea's decision to pull out of denuclearization talks with the US. Furthermore, the French and Germany governments reported that their domestic manufacturing contracted further in March, driving the benchmark ten-year German government bond yield below zero and adding to fears of a global slowdown in growth. Additionally, all of Europe was looming under the constant fear and uncertainty that the Brexit departure would cause a European recession, as all of the economies were tied to the euro's value and the uncertainty of a major contributor withdrawing from the treaty. This threat loomed so heavily that on March 25, 2019, with only one week left to consummate a deal, the British Government took control of the Brexit negotiations from the Prime Minister Teresa May's authority, as all confidence in her abilities to find a resolution agreement with the EU had been lost.

Additionally, three days later the Muller Report would be concluded, revealing whether or not the Trump Administration colluded with the Russian Government to rig the US Presidential Election in 2016, which resulted in Donald

Trump being the forty-fifth president of the United States. In my opinion, the Muller Report was a complete waste of resources and time. Robert Muller had no choice but to exonerate President Trump of collusion if for nothing else but the welfare of the nation. If the Muller Report had stated the democratic process of the Republic for which America stands had been subverted, the nation would probably collapsed under military control and instantaneously revert into a dictatorship thereby throwing the free world into turmoil. How else would a nation that thought it controlled its own destiny respond if they were to find out that they themselves overthrown and hoodwinked into being a dictatorship by proxy? If nothing else, President Trump's admission during a televised interview to firing the director of the FBI James Comey, for investigating him and his relationship with the Russians, is and was the definition of obstruction of justice. Firing an investigator to prevent them from learning and revealing your actions is an obstruction, and the main stream media ignoring the obstruction is just as criminal as the perpetrator himself. Fast forward to 1 May 2019, and the US Attorney General William Barr admitted that he used his prosecutorial discretion to exonerate President Trump of obstruction of justice charges prior to releasing the Muller Report to the public. One key note is using one's prosecutorial discretion does not mean they are exonerated but it just won't be prosecuted.

Like it or not the world is headed for a recession, and all the play callers know it. This is exactly why the Federal Reserve cut its quantitative tightening initiative short and froze interest rates in an unprecedented move for a year and a half. Additionally, Trump's trickle down economic tax plan gave large tax breaks to the wealthiest of Americans at the expense of the middle class failed. Every society survives on the backs of the middle classes. The rich avoid paying taxes as much as they can via loopholes and creative accounting, and the poor have nothing to contribute, but demand more, from those who have more. Hence is why it's the middle class that supports any economy.

I wouldn't be surprised if all the developed nations were in collusion, keeping us distracted with recessions and hostilities that will never develop into a World War III as they try to figure out how to handle the alien dilemma. COVID-19 would be a brilliant way to get people to volunteer for a vaccination; if it works, it would allow human and an alien race to cohabitate on a planet. As recently as April 2019, the US Air Force and navy developed a joint UFO, or as the new term goes "UAP," Unexplained Aerial Phenomena program to track, explain, or determine the intent of the phenomena. Sure, some voiceless poor people will die during the distractions, more than likely they'll be Syrian, Iraqi, Iranian, African, or some poor South American immigrant, but those are all poor people are easily sacrificed for a few bucks (cynicism). In today's technological age, with information being instantly available through various social media outlets, authorities no longer have the ability to control, suppress, or deny otherworldly events as they did in the past.

As a society, one of the worst things we've done is to allow others to gather and disseminate data for us, thereby sanctioning them to control what we see and hear. We have become so distracted and busy we no longer read or do our own research but merely listen to the radio or look at the TV and take what we see or hear "as the gospel" from the biblical Prophet Paul, never questioning whether or not is there more to the story. This is exactly why CNN and Fox News have completely opposite views but neither network tells you the news.

One obvious sign that we are being purposely distracted is not the headlining event but the ancillary news on the back page or on page two of the major newspapers, where they casually mention the life-altering occurrence like the national crime bill passing in the mid-nineties after the Oklahoma City bombing, or during the controversially fired FBI director James Comey Senate hearing in June 2017, the US Congress, on the very same day across the street, completed another step in the repeal of the Dodd Frank Financial Reform Act of 2010, which was developed and implemented to prevent another housing initiated financial crisis like the one endured just a few years prior.

Another example of the public being distracted was the 1980s African famine. As the world was focused on millions of Africans starving and musical artists wrote and sang songs to bring resources and attention to the tragedy, the AIDS epidemic had quietly creeped its way in and woven itself into the fabric of society as a deadly infectious disease.

As the US Center for Disease Control and the World Health Organization (WHO) mobilized and went to Africa and provided inoculation to the masses, AIDS/HIV came to the forefront as well; some may see this as a false coincidence as I do. A coincidence is not when opportunity and preparation meets, which is just the case here. I believe this scenario was orchestrated to take advantage of and test a biological weapon designed in a laboratory made to be a doomsday backup plan, if in the case of all-out war, whereas one country could make their enemy's army too sick to fight and weaken their resolve. Or perhaps AIDS/HIV was created in a lavatory to prevent humans from being infected by alien antigens from our cosmic neighbors that crashed in our backyard in July 1947, and previously in other countries, but went unpublicized by other nations. Even more so perhaps COVID-19 is the second human trial for AIDS/HIV immunization. I accept this as true because HIV/AIDS is a retrovirus, which is one of only three known retroviruses because it doesn't naturally occur in nature. Do your own research, just don't take my word. Initially, we were told AIDS/HIV occurred because of gay males having sex, and in Africa because they were practicing bestiality, having sex with primates. However, if AIDS/HIV came from gay men and bestiality, why didn't Caligula, the Roman emperor from AD 37 until AD 41, have it? The disease surely would have survived through the ages as it has no known cure and people were not as sanitary then as they are now. However, of the thirty-four million HIV-positive people worldwide, 69 percent live in Africa and an estimated 66 percent of gay men are HIV positive. Coincidently, these two groups along with the poor are the most discriminated clusters in society (minorities and gays).

This vaguely reminds me of when in 1946–48 the US CDC intentionally infected over thirteen hundred Guatemalans with syphilis, gonorrhea, and chancroid and conducted serology test on them and others. Some of the victims were even institutionalized mental patients; some may believe this was an anomaly, but during the Tuskegee syphilis experiment, four hundred Black men were left untreated for forty years from 1932 until 1972, so government doctors could study the course of the disease. Even then the study only ended because journalists exposed it, creating a public outcry, and by then over one hundred men had already died from the disease.

The easiest way to make people surrender their liberties is to present the alternative of doom and gloom through fear and the possibilities of damage and destruction if submission is not immediately granted. Take for example the events following September 11, 2001, when as a collective society we saw red, and retribution was the only solution. Even though fifteen of the nineteen hijackers were Saudi Arabian and we were told that they trained in Afghanistan, the US military response was to send twenty-five thousand troops to Afghanistan and 250,000 troops to Iraq, a country not mentioned anywhere in the equation. Worst of all, the homeland and host country of the majority of hijackers was not only let off the hook but rewarded with huge contracts for logistical support and staging of US troops. Perhaps the first country that should have gotten the Tomahawk cruise missile shower is Saudi Arabia? Instead, it was the small godforsaken, desolate country of Afghanistan, and the oil rich nation of Iraq, and the very media whose job it is to ask the tough questions and keep the public informed not only said nothing but had no questions either.

Since the media didn't ask the hard-hitting questions, and even worse, said nothing, I will tell you what I speculate occurred. I surmise in some dimly lit room some very rich men drinking some very expensive Scotch conspired a plan to increase their personal wealth at the expense of the American public and Armed Forces. I further speculate that these rich and powerful individuals were well connected to the individuals who manage the inner working of the US Government and knew exactly whom they needed to contact and whom they could trust in order for this charade to be pulled off. Iraq was invaded for its readily available and plentiful oil reserves, and Saddam Hussain's resistance to being a CIA Middle East puppet. Furthermore, the technology to recover the vast North American oil sand reserves was either nonexistent or cost prohibitive in relation to oil industry profit margins.

Therefore, Iraq, an old Middle East ally, was turned into a new enemy as big business used their political influence to set the conditions necessary for an invasion of a small country that posed no physical threat to the developed world but did seek to control its life's blood, which was a majority of the world's accessible oil reserves. Iraq's invasion of its small, oil-rich neighbor, Kuwait, whom they accused of slant drilling and stealing oil from them near their shared boarder, if gone unchecked would have given Iraq control of the lion's share of the world's known and easily accessible petroleum reserves. Petroleum's vast uses are not limited to gasoline but also used in the manufacturing of plastic, paints, pesticides, polyurethane wood products, and rubber production to name a few things. If one country was allowed to corner the marked on this substance, they would in turn be allowed to hold the developed world at its mercy by controlling production and prices of this vital elixir and any derivatives from it.

Any attempt to corner the market of such a vital natural resource is a direct threat to the sovereignty of any nation that requires the substance to sustain life as they know it; therefore, it becomes a matter of national security that must be dealt with swiftly. Many will say that Iraq was not invaded for its oil, but no other plausible reason exist for the conflict. Of the twenty-eight-nation member countries of NATO, Kuwait was not and is not a NATO member; although meek, it had its own military and offered nothing else of value but its ability to produce oil, and at a very cheap cost, which was desperately needed to keep America's and Western European countries' industries growing.

Conversely, Kuwait is a member of the United Nations; however, this was not a UN-sanctioned operation to protect the citizens of one of its member countries, as the UN does peacekeeping and nation-building, not offensive military responses.

Afghanistan was invaded for the estimated one trillion dollars of rare earth minerals deposits it sits upon, which is in everything from cellphones, gorilla glass to computer chips. Rare earth elements are the new platinum, and the much-needed material for development of future technology. Rare earth elements are a group of seventeen chemically similar elements crucial to the manufacturing of many high tech products such as superconductors, powerful pulsed lasers, cancer treatment drugs, rheumatoid arthritis medicines, and surgical supplies to name a few things. Afghanistan sits on one of the world's largest deposits of rare earth elements, and the government and people are too disorganized, poor, and concerned about daily survival to capitalize on it. This is why the Soviet Union invaded Afghanistan in the eighties, and we (the US) supplied them the means of resistance. The Soviets tried to take the resources by force, and the US tried to take them by subversion, posing as a friend, and now the Chinese as a business partners.

A secondary reason given for the invasion of Afghanistan was its production poppies, which the main ingredient in cocaine and opium production. However, as the laws of supply and demand dictate, they are only producing what is in demand. The Western world cannot solve their recreational and casual drug use problems by killing the supply, because as long as there is a demand, there will be someone willing to supply it, which will only drive up the price and create correlational spike in crime as users become more desperate to acquire the necessary resources to support their addictions. The Western world must solve their drug dependence issues by eliminating the demand, thereby the supply will not be desired or required, this being a problem that would fix itself. Besides, most of the Western world's cocaine supply comes from South America, not Afghanistan; Afghanistan cocaine supply goes to Europe.

On a side note, the US drug problem is, in my opinion, not only self-inflicted but also is a great option for population control. Drugs are one of the few things that governments can use to employ all three of their control measures at one time. Illegal drugs have the ability to distract, appease, and suppress you at the same time, much like religion and relationships. Now if you look at a country the size of the US, which spans from coast to coast, any consumable product that is readily available in any region at relatively the same price needs a well-established distribution systems to keep the product immediately available.

The US mainland is approximately 3.12 million square miles; even if we as a nation are only using half of our land mass and the rest is unpopulated, that still would require someone to supply 1.56 million square miles with consumable drugs on a constant bases. Now this distribution system would have to mirror the supply chains of major petroleum distributors, grocery stores, and the US postal service to keep its customers supplied with a disposable product that requires replenishment after usage. Now let's think. Who or what has the resources and ability and can run an operation of this magnitude for decades with impunity? FedEx, Walmart, Shell petroleum?

Yes, all of these organizations have that capability, but this is a prohibited product, and transporting it would be illegal and is not worth the hassle or risking the billions they make of legitimate sales annually. However, the US military has the same capability (distribution points): military bases in every region of the country and posts up and down both coast and the Gulf of Mexico, the planes, ships, trucks, and logistical capability to do the same thing, and all they would have to do is label the cargo as classified or top secret and no one would or could question the cargo, or verify that they are moving what they said it is, or its final destinations.

Now I'm not accusing the US military of knowingly trafficking drugs; they could merely be following orders. For those who question my logic, there is evidence of the CIA introducing drugs into South Central LA in the eighties, and no one wanted believe that initially as well. (Excuse me, as I digressed, so back to Afghanistan...)

Although Afghanistan had become a safe haven for the Taliban and other extremists at the time of the 2001 US military invasion, it lacked the ability and desire to exert its fanatical philosophy on the rest of the world. Even if Afghanistan was a sanctuary for Bin Laden, it is very hard to justify a full on military assault verses a surgical strike team whose mission would be to capture or kill the 9/11 mastermind. However, as it turns out, Bin Laden was hiding in plain sight less than a mile away from the Pakistani's Government equivalent to the US army's West Point Military Academy. I distinctly remember Presidents Bush's address to the nation when he stated no boarders of the harboring country would be respected in our hunt for the mastermind of the despicable act portrayed on our nation as we sought (vengeance) justice for those that were murdered, and how we would make no distinction between Bin Laden and those who harbored him.

Bin Laden's presence and location in Pakistan surely must have been known by Pakistani officials, and yet they said nothing, which in my opinion makes them an enemy of the state as well. Additionally, this is why the Obama Administration would rather risk a war and did not notify the Pakistani officials of the impending covert mission crossing into their sovereign territory to capture or kill Bin Laden as they knew they could not be trusted. However,

Pakistan was not only let off the hook for harboring the world's most wanted terrorist but rewarded with logistical support contracts and foreign aid for allowing the US military to move war-ready materials and supplies through their country in route to Afghanistan, while, I believe, this was in some ways an appeasement for the previous sovereignty violation.

The World Trade Center's Twin Towers collapsed within thirty minutes of one another in what appeared to be controlled explosions.

Simultaneously, President George W. Bush appeared to be reading a book upside down to a group of first-graders in Florida. Perhaps Bush holding the book upside down (as seen in the Michael Moore's film *Fahrenheit 9/11*) was a subliminal signal to the country of him being in distress, much like when the US flag being flown upside down? I think President Bush was emotionally and physically paralyzed that these events had come to fruition and he was powerless to stop them.

President Bush's no immediate response spoke louder than any words he could have mustered. Being one of the most powerful men in the world, and the sitting president when these horrific attacks were perpetrated, when informed of the then "evident terror attacks" and overt act of war, the president didn't move, and I believe this is because he knew what was going to happen before it happened. As much prestige and power the US president has, at the end of the day they are just figureheads, much like the Queen of England or Emperor of Japan. The fact of the matter is the president is just the face representing the nation in a temporary job that they will be removed from in four to eight years, or sooner via elections or impeachment if warranted. I think the US is not managed by the person or persons and their staffs we think we elected but by a shadow government for stability purposes, program management, and population control, and national elections are mere appeasements to keep the natives at bay.

Further analysis regarding the events of September 11th, 2001, leads me to the conclusion of the virtual statistical impossibility of the Twin Towers to collapse the way that they did less than thirty minutes apart of one another as they were struck by planes on different floors, at different speeds, at different times. Furthermore, we were told that the fuel that leaked from the crashed airliners superheated the steel that supported the Trade Centers structures' foundation, and that's why the buildings collapsed the way they did. However, can you comprehend how many of gallons of fuel it would have taken to get from where the planes impacted the buildings to the foundations of the WTC's, to not only pool but ignite, burn, and sustain a fire intense enough that could destroy a building of that size? Just as thought-provoking, no wings or tail was recovered from the plane that hit the Pentagon roughly thirty minutes later, 250 miles away, as these more frangible components attached to the main body of the fuselage should have sheared off.

Even more remarkable, the third plane hit a part of the Pentagon that just happen to be being renovated, as "luck" would have it, minimizing destruction and loss of life. Perhaps the most interesting revelation from all of these events is when, for the first time in US aviation history, the FAA (Federal Aviation Administration) instituted its ATC zero emergency plan, whereas all national airspace was shut down and all airborne planes had to land immediately at the nearest available airport and no departures were allowed. During all this madness and uncertainty, the president of the United States allowed three privately charted planes with approximately 140 Saudi Royal family members and their friends to leave the country on private jets without being questioned by the FBI as to their knowledge of the events and their whereabouts on the days before and morning of the tragic events. Not to mention some of the passengers were directly related to Bin Laden himself, the supposed mastermind of the horrific event.

Have you noticed that the US military is always looking for an enemy? For the longest time it was communism, i.e., the Viet Cong, the Cubans, followed by the Korean War, the Sandinistas in Nicaragua, Panama invasion, then the Middle East wars, in the mid-nineties the fall of communism, back to the Middle East and the Iranians, Yemen, then back to the Russians being our enemy, and now China and North Korea are foes as well. As I've said before, the governments use these diversions and hostilities to distract you from the real agenda because they don't think you can handle the truth. I believe the most important thing you can do for yourself is to educate yourself not only in the things that interest you but also the things that don't.

As I see it, you will naturally gravitate towards your interests, but the things that you don't know will do the most harm to you, and often times these things are right before you.

Science tells us that the universe is expanding at the rate of 46.2 plus or minus 1.3 miles per mega parsec, or roughly three million light years per second, in all directions, and the universe is approximately 13.8 billion years old, but how do we know this? If space is expanding, what is it expanding into, and when it stops expanding, will it then contract? Thereby compressing into itself and imploding under its own pressure? Another way of contemplating this is, the universe is expanding at a rate of 558 billion miles per second in all directions, and the estimated size of the universe is ninety-three billion light years, with a known size of forty-six billion light years, while light travels at 186,000 miles per second. Perhaps our concept of time is wrong? Perhaps we are at the beginning stages of the creation explosion and that's why the universe is expanding, kind of like when a firecracker first explodes. Maybe what we consider to be millions of years of time is actually merely the first milliseconds of an actual explosion? Much like a mayfly that has the lifespan of approximately one day, that day is actually a lifetime for the fly but merely a brief moment in time for us. How far, high, and wide is the universe, and where is the bottom of space? Where does the Earth fit in the universe; is it at the center, edge, or top or bottom of the universe? How many galaxies exist in the cosmos? Where does the universe begin and end? And most interesting, what preceded the universe's existence? Furthermore, recent discoveries bring to question the Hubble Constant and the possibility that the universe is expanding faster than previously thought, thereby bringing into question the true age of the universe once again. The Bible implies that the Earth is approximately six thousand years old by using contextual clues of the Masoretic Hebrew text of Genesis 5 and 11. Furthermore, Spanish, Chinese, Egyptian, Persian, Babylonian, Anglo-Saxons, British, Irish, the Vatican, and even Mayan cultures all fall within a three-thousand-year variable on the Earth's age, varying between 3113 BC till current. However, if we believe science, life on Earth started about 3.82 billion years ago, but what happened in the universe the ten billion years prior to microbiological earthly existence? Surely, in almost fourteen billion years we are not the only life the universe has produced. And if all of these numbers are even remotely close, what happen to the dinosaurs that ruled the Earth for millions of years before man's dominion?

What if on July 3, 1947, concrete proof of other life in the universe crashed landed right in humanity's back yard? Not on the front lawn of the White House, but on a sheep ranch outside of Roswell New Mexico, only to be discovered and denied five days later by the rancher and the US Army Air Corps? Do you really think the commander of the Roswell Army Air Corp Base would not have known of a clandestine balloon test going on the installation he commanded? Furthermore, even if he had not been informed for security reasons, he surely would have been educated on any such project before a press release had been authorized announcing the existence of other worldly beings. I speculate the top-secret weather balloon test story was a lie, and not only was the existence of other life in the universe confirmed but a deliberate and devious plot was formulated to deny the event, the existence of alien survivors, and the technology harvested from it. If the US Army Air Corps had stuck to its original press release, the rest of world would have insisted on the US Government sharing what it found and learned of and from our cosmic neighbors, and the US would then lose any technological advantages it was seeking.

Furthermore, this recent civilization-altering discovery showed just how unprepared we were to defend ourselves and our planet from the alien callers, and since we had no clue of the intent of our visitors, it was best to just keep quiet. From that moment on, I speculate that US authorities knew big changes were in store for mankind, and more than anything the US wanted to be at the forefront, not to mention no other nations at that time had admitted what they had known of or knew about aliens either, so why should we share?

So I hypothesize, for these reasons, less than seventy days later on September 18th, 1947, the US Air Force was established with a covert primary mission and directives to find out the visitors capabilities and intentions, and figure out a way to defend the planet if necessary. (Conversely, the reason why the US navy operates its own Naval Air Corps is because US Air Force's true mission is alien investigations, as proven by projects Blue Book, Project Sign, and various other unacknowledged projects in attempts to explain the undeniable.) Knowing there was no way for mankind to defeat or defend against such a technologically advanced race, our leadership at the time agreed to concession to appease the aliens, but to also buy us time to strategize a defense. In return for our cooperation and submission, the extraterrestrials provide us with advanced technology beyond our wildest dreams, and this is exactly why ninety-seven days after the Air Force was established, Chuck Yeager broke the sound barrier at 767 miles per hour. How else can you explain man's technological advances from 1903's man's first flight aloft at Kitty Hawk for fifty-nine seconds and 852 feet to 1969 with a man landing on the moon 239,000 miles away and returning to the Earth safely, a round trip of approximately 478,000 miles? In these amazing accomplishment, which took roughly sixty-six years, equivalent to a millisecond of human existence, our species went from just out of living in caves to putting a man on the moon.

For example, perhaps they gave us the ability to split the atom and make endless energy, but we weaponized it and made the nuclear bombs. Perhaps they gave us the cure for cancer, but we kitted it away and sold it to only the wealthiest of individuals to help finance the scientific programs and continued to let the masses die.

This was about the same time that people stopped inventing things and corporations started doing so. When you research who invented the most important discoveries in the earliest part of the last century, like telephones, computers, and TVs, a person will be credited, but in the later part of the same century, it's always a corporation, and this is part of the deception.

For example, when looking at the integrated circuit chip, to a layman it looks more like Morse code or a collage of dots and dashes that carry data. But one must ask why anyone would think dots and dashes of silver would be the perfect conduit to carry data and electrical signals on a plastic wafer board instead of a simple of wire?

This robust new organization would need unlimited resources in its quest for understanding and must appear to be in the legitimate business of defending our nation, not hunting for aliens. The resources to fund this campaign would be allocated from Congress through the budgetary process and black budgets that don't appear on any ledger, and additional funds would come in the form of severe overpayments for things like hammers, aircraft, and innocuous purchases like toilet seats, nuts, and bolts. For example, do you really think the US government would pay one billion dollars each for forty B2 bombers or 123 million dollars each for 400 F-35 fighter jet or 122 million dollars each for eighty new Marine transport helicopters? In a nation of approximately 330 million people, of which 165 million actually contribute to federal coffers, with the other 165 million being either too young, too old to work, too indigent to pay taxes, incarcerated, or saddled with an illegal immigration status.

Consequently, the average American actually owes the US Government the equivalent of a new Mercedes-Benz, approximately fifty-four thousand dollars, (as of this writing) to pay off their part of national debt, and that number increases daily due to interest.

The second stage of a two-prong defense from alien visitors is to immunize ourselves from any alien-borne pathogens. COVID-19 (example). In order to protect people from a threat that they don't know exists, you must convince them to accept treatment without them being told what they are being treated for. The best way to do this is through fear of being infected or sickened by a known but incurable disease or vaccinations to prevent a pandemic or future disability such as polio, MMR, or cervical cancer. Have you noticed the alarming uptick in autism, cancers, peanut allergies, and attention deficit disorder (ADD)? When I was a kid, autism was a rarity to nonexistent, and ADD was cured with a spanking, and everyone ate peanut butter and jelly sandwiches. So the primary question is, what causes the increases in occurrences?

I speculate the medical industries and food production systems have been used as unwitting facilitators fulfilling their rolls in the program to vaccinate mankind from possible interbreeding or planet sharing with unearthly beings. Have you noticed that indigent and poor people are the who receive no to minimal prenatal care have the healthiest babies? This brings to mind the biblical saying in Mathew 5.5 the meek shall inherit the earth.

I accept this as true and correlate this to the lack of health care access or modern medicine intervention into their pregnancies; correspondingly, those who attend all the prenatal appointments and seek access to the best health care have the highest percentage of children in the autistic spectrum.

There is fact based conjecture that in 2004 the US Center for Disease Control (CCD) conducted a study on the measles, mumps, rubella (MMR) vaccination causing autism, and they purportedly destroyed and manipulated the data that did not support the outcome they wanted, and yet they have continued to support and enforce mass distribution of inoculations knowing the possible negative outcome of an increased probability and likely autism development if administered at the age of eighteen months instead of waiting until three to four years of age.

There is even a 2012 CNN report, which states the CDC's own study concluding a 78 percent increase in autism from 2002 to 2012, with boys being more prone to develop the disease than girls. Even more interesting, this phenomena is not just limited to the US, France experienced similar issues in the early 1990s when aluminum hydroxide adjuvant from a vaccine remained embedded in the muscle tissue, thereby causing a disorder called MMF.

Also when Germany increased inoculations from six to thirty-four vaccinations since 1934, they also saw an increase in child illnesses such as cancers, allergies, ADD, ADHD, and rheumatism. So, again, one must ask why, fully knowing the likely conclusion would the CDCs of different nations, force this likely fate upon small innocent children? I can only surmise, by not knowing all the facts, the probable alternative would be a much worse option. Moreover, the UK and Canada also saw similar defect results with their inoculation programs as well when vaccinations increased.

At a time when medical miracles and advancement are being discovered faster than any other time in history, we appear to be going backwards in these areas or stagnated at best. (If you noticed anyone who refuses to inoculate themselves or their children is labeled a possible public health risk and ostracized from the public-school systems that they are forced to pay into via taxes? Social pressure is a soft tactic to rein in the not fully committed resisters or the unsure.) (So, is COVID-19 the cause or the failed cure? Is the possible vaccine a godsend or the devil's blend?) Additionally, I believe the very food we purchase for consumption is being genetically altered to account for any rebels or stragglers not willing to be immunized and inoculated thereby avoiding the system.

Hence is why pre-adolescent children are physically developing at a much earlier stages than in past generations. What's more, who will care for all the autistic children once they are physically mature but mentally underdeveloped and their primary caregiver passes on? Often, when a responsible person or couple has a special needs child, they tend not to have other children but focus their time and resources on providing the best care they can for their child born with unexpected additional expenses. As a result of this, when that or those primary caregivers pass on, there is no one left to assume the obligation, and the disabled end up homeless. So the logical questions is, is society prepared to see the increase in disabled, helpless, and/or handicapped individuals out on the streets unable to fend for themselves? It is also safe to assume that if the extraterrestrial beings are exploring our planet, they want our planetary resources, as no other planets in our solar system has trees, liquid water, or an atmosphere like Earth's. Perchance the visitors are interested in experimenting with interbreeding our two species to ensure survival of theirs, or maybe perhaps even ours, as we are destroying this planet at an alarming rate.

Perhaps they are arranging for us to leave this planet before we can no longer survive on it, and they must biologically prepare us for the pending journey, but this preparation will take several human generations to be complete.

In the Hebrew Bible, it speaks of Methuselah having lived 969 years, but with lifespans of this length no longer being an option, generational biological adaptation is the only option. Perhaps the extraterrestrial beings have a better understanding of time and space than we do and they are preparing us to leave this planet before a future event destroys life as we know it, like what possibly happened to the dinosaurs? As irrational as this sounds, our earliest ancestors left us plenty of unexplainable ancient structures as breadcrumbs to forewarn us of cultural resets. The ruins of Machu Picchu, Puma Punku, Tiwanaku Tinwanaku, the Great Pyramids, Göbekli Tepe in southern Turkey, and Easter Island all defy man's known abilities at those times to achieve building such momentous structures. Even with today's best heavy equipment using hydraulics as a primary lifting force, we are still unable to duplicate most of their efforts to this day.

These relics were designed and erected with such precision it indicates that ancient man had assistance with planning and executing such complex edifices. One must also wonder what happen to the societies that built such structures. Did they just die off? How and why were these successful building techniques abandoned?

All things seem to indicate that man's time and earthly knowledge was reset for some reason. If this is not the case, should we not be technologically light years ahead of where we are now?

You are constantly asked to believe what you are told, not your lying eyes. For example, during the March 1997 Phoenix light event, thousands of people witnessed a purported V-shaped UFO approximately one mile in diameter; several even had the wherewithal to record video evidence, and yet they were told that their eyes deceived them and that they should believe the government and Air Force's explanation of A-10s returning from the Barry Goldwater training ranges that had in avertedly dropped flares all at the same time.

The problem with this rendition is A-10 aircraft engines make noise, and this one-mile-wide craft was silent; furthermore, A-10s and all military aircraft are prohibited from dropping flares over populated areas. So the question now becomes, why would five A-10s flying in a V formation drop flares over a major Southwest city? And why where they flying in a V-shaped formation (which, by the way, they never do), when the standard formation flight is two aircraft flying abreast of one another? Even as recently as 2019 the US Navy and Air Force created a joint program to study the unexplained phenomena.

What if mankind was created by aliens as a form of AI? Perhaps, humans are the original artificial intelligence (AI), and the reason time seems to be restarted is because we became too advanced and aware, which is a fear we currently face with the AI we've created. Perhaps the North Star followed by the three wise men was a UFO guiding them to Joseph and Mary? Perhaps since Mary was a virgin, the baby Jesus was a product of artificial insemination. Maybe this is why the Catholic Church can inexcusably allow priests to go from parish to parish molesting little boys and why Christians feel free to use faith and religion to exploit money from their members and the Muslims find it perfectly okay to use violence as they seek peace. I think these three major religions and governments alike use religion as a means of societal self-policing. If the government was to proclaim God is an alien, and there is no Heaven or Hell, there would be no reason to secure a place for your soul in the afterlife. People being free of retribution for their actions would promulgate anarchies for many. Furthermore, some aspects of religion just does not pass the rational test. For example, why would such a loving, forgiving, and benevolent God condemn you to Hell for all of eternity for the less than a hundred years you spend on earth?

Wouldn't it be more logical that you were condemned for an equal period of time that you lived and reigned hell on earth? Also, what about those innocents who die and never got to live a meaningful life or a life at all? Or, as the saying goes, everything that happens is part of God's plan? So are you now saying that God planned for horrific things to happen for some people? Was it God's plan for some people to be murdered, kidnapped, raped, or hooked on drugs or babies aborted? In all of God's glory and astir, and of all the life he has created, the billions and trillion of souls and beings, why does he see fit to care about you a single grain of sand? So, is it narcissistic to believe you matter to God, or is it acknowledgement to accept that you were created for a divine purpose and your work is not done yet. For a long time my anger, arrogance, and disappointment allowed me to presume Jesus, the Tooth Fairy, and Santa Claus were all of equal standing. I felt that way because, as a Black man, I saw no reason to believe in an entity like Jesus, after all the suffering that Blacks had endured throughout time. I wondered how such a loving and caring God could allow such anguish and destruction of one tribe. However, I come to realize the misery that Africans and all of their descendants has endured was and is a necessary evil. I believe Blacks are and have always been part of the chosen tribe. Blacks have not been forgotten or abandoned by God but, on the contrary, are being prepared for their place in heaven and on the throne. The suffering is necessary because as with many things not earned, they are not appreciated. I believe that most people could not or would not enjoy heaven and paradise without knowing the torment of hell. For example, have you ever seen people waste or not take the best care of things they themselves did not work for? It is human nature to appreciate what they've worked for and earned, and just being given things does not evoke the level of appreciation necessary. As the old saying goes, "you don't miss the water until the well goes dry." When the Bible speaks of wandering the wilderness for forty years, I believe the time table is relative. For example, are we talking forty dog years, forty human years, or forty God years, which may very well be four thousand human years? Getting to heaven without sacrifice would make heaven hell. Heaven would be full of malcontent spirits wailing and complaining about paradise. From Earth to the observable edge of the universe is 46.5 billion light years, but what is beyond that what we can see? After the body dies, what happens to the soul or spirit? Does it go back into the guff (the Hebrew repository of souls)?

My grandmother used to say, "a half truth is a whole lie," which makes me question several aspects of religion. Case in point: in the King James Version of the Bible, the names Mary, Joseph, Jesus, and many other names just don't fit in with the biblical depiction of the region of these historic events. Why do the people have such Europeancentric names in the heart of the Middle East at the beginning of modern history? Perhaps Yahweh is the heavenly father's name of the child born to the virgin and her husband, but with the stroke of a pen and a royal decree, King James changed the name from Mahammad to Jesus. The European followers could then relate to the story and have an ancestral claim, thereby making the story relatable, believable, and acceptable. After all, who dare question the king, and with all other versions destroyed, how could one do so?

During the time of the Crusades, Christianity was imposed upon any culture the British and European forces encountered, while, simultaneously, countless alternative deities' belief structures were dismantled. Another case in point, the Mayans, Greeks, Vikings, and Egyptians. Through different periods of time, all worshiped various gods and gave voluminous thanks to the many deities for the blessings they received. This even included the Native Northern Americans, who recognized various spirits and acknowledged their contributions to their daily lives. However, the Christians only worshiped one God—and in their eyes, that god provided everything they needed. Prior to the invasion of Africa by the Europeans, the African people worshiped Allah, and the singular religion was Muslim, which remains for many on the African continent still today. Several centuries later, the dispersed descendants of those Africans now share the Christian belief structure and worship the "Son of God, a mortal Jesus Christ" made of flesh and blood for man to postulate. Moreover, a built-up distain for Muslims and Islam and has since developed, and people openly view them as an enemy and treat them as terrorists, not the brothers and sisters or children born from the same heavenly father. There appears to be a very concerted misinformation campaign design to silence alternate deity worships. So, if King James changed names as to make the stories more acceptable, that makes his biblical depiction a whole lie not a half truth. This leads me to question, what else did he change? Don't get me wrong, the Bible is a great life guide and excellent source of direction when you are lost or seeking knowledge and understanding, but it may just be a lot of "his stories"... and not history, and by the way, the devil probably has a voice too.

So now I'm fathoming, possibly, is this your last chance? Perhaps your current existence is an opportunity for you to right all the wrongs you've done in past lives—and this is your final opportunity before an eternity in hell swimming in the lake of fire? Perchance this existence is purgatory, and you've already squandered the last opportunity to save your pitiful soul, and this is the train to hell, your personal transport arriving next at the eternal damnation station? My confidence in documented history is shaken, and my belief in man waivers at best. There seems to be no rational narrative to explain man's existence, purpose, or survival over previous apex predators, which accounts for all the possible outcomes of an individual's choices. Complicating matters even further, there are forces at work that exceed my limited ability to comprehend the mediums in which I must operate and the ones that surround me. Happenings such as paranormal activity, numerology, karma, psychic abilities, apparitions, remote viewing, multiple dimensions, or unrested souls defy conventional logic, leading me back to the realm of faith and belief. For now I'll just hang my hat on being a good person and doing right by others.

As a Black man, I would be remised if I didn't address universal oppression the descendants of Africa have experienced throughout the years and the world. Some may wonder why I did not use the more accepted phrase of African American; I chose not to use this phase because the persecution, prejudice, and discrimination experienced by persons of African descent is universal from Europe to Asia, South America, even the Middle East. The darker your skin the more likely you are to be persecuted or discriminated against. Blacks and/or African Americans are the most imitated, feared, and yet misunderstood of all the races I've encountered; their style, music, attitude, and athleticism are emulated throughout the world, but they are yet to be accepted universally and unconditionally for who they are.

Blacks appear to all be lumped into the categories, of athlete, entertainers, criminals, lazy, or poor; we are not afforded the presumptions of being professionals, doctors, lawyers, or any other prestigious title upon first encounters. For hundreds of years people of African descent have been enslaved, murdered, and degraded, thereby destroying their very foundation of humanity or being deserving of it. The practice of slavery on the descendants from Africa, although most well-known because of the North American history, was perpetrated and promulgated throughout the world, but slowly abolished one country at a time.

For example, slavery was abolished in England in 1808, and in the US in 1865 via the Thirteenth Amendment; however, Brazil was the last country in the Western world to emancipate its slaves in 1888. For a period of about one hundred years, the world slowly came to terms that no human being should be owned by another. With hair of wool and skin of bronze Blacks have endured more persecution than any other race in history; some may say Jews have endured just as much but via the biblical description. Jews and Blacks share the same characteristics and origins, thereby being one in the same.

Although slavery was slowly abolished throughout the world, prejudice and ignorance still reigned supreme via segregation, separate but equal policies, colorism, and Jim Crow laws. This institutionalized ignorance substituted one form of discrimination and suppression for another. If the Fifteenth Amendment gave Black men the right to vote in 1869, why was it necessary ninety years later for the 1960 Civil Rights Act and the 1965 Voting Rights Acts? Answer: your vote doesn't count, and it stopped counting in 1869 for poor whites and Blacks. The only reason the right to vote was given was because, at that point, they, the powers that be, decided that those votes wouldn't count anyway, but it would appease the natives and keep the peace.

The continuous disassembling of families during slavery via the slave owners selling off parents and children continues to effect modern African descendants to this day. According to a recent Census survey, about half of all Black children in the US live in single-parent households, where their primary caregiver had full or partial custody.

The Census Bureau explains that the proportion of Black children who lives with their custodial parent while their other parent lives outside their household is about twice as many as the proportion of white children. Among parents who have child support agreements, less than half actually receive the full amount of support they're entitled to.

For hundreds of years Blacks were not allowed to be a family unit, constantly being broken apart and controlled by violence and fear with no input into their own destiny.

Once the slaves was granted their freedom via the Thirteenth Amendment, they were free to go but had nowhere to go and no means to get there. The dilemma placed them in a unique and uncomfortable position ripe for exploitation called sharecropping. Sharecropping basically was indentured servitude or voluntary slavery; having no revenue to buy the tools they needed to farm the land they tended, the ex-slaves were forced to purchase the apparatuses from the owner of the land they worked. The tools were sold to the free men and women at prices so high the equipment would break or wear out before being paid off, thereby incurring more debt, legally and morally enslaving them.

In addition, many with no other skills, not even the ability to read, what options or opportunities did they have? Moving forward to more modern times, for various reason persons of African descent, especially in America, still experience reverberation from their ancestors struggles. The lack of generational history still appears to stifle the culture. In America, Blacks or persons of African descent are more likely to be undereducated, poor, and/or incarcerated. I believe the primary reasons for this is systematic racism are stop and frisk, possession laws, under-education and standardized testing, the broken home environment, and lack of a constructive influential male in the home, or perhaps the mantra of women continuously repeating and speaking into existence ("I don't need a man"). See, when a woman repeatedly states that "she doesn't need a man," she doesn't get a man; she seeks and finds a male. In turn she ends up with a male that will only procreate, not a man who will take care of his obligations and the responsibilities he creates. Moreover, in 1964, President Lyndon B. Johnson introduced a series of legislation known as the War on Poverty in response to a persistently high poverty rate, around 20 percent. He funded programs such as Social Security, and welfare programs, food stamps, job corps, and Head Start. This was also the beginning of the great decline in the Black family, when it was more financially advantageous for the man not to be present in the home with the woman and his children in order for them to receive public assistance if they needed help. This placed the woman in the position of being sole provider and created a hyena effect family social dynamic, consequently, the dominate role model in her children's lives. Public assistance allowed the Black family to survive but not thrive, and with the absence of a strong male role model, the Black woman had to step up and fill those shoes too. This was a great example for little Black girls of what a woman can accomplish, but for little Black boys, this subconsciously taught them to be submissive to women, and that his presence was not necessary for the family's survival or not necessarily a key component of the family unit. These little footnotes will more than likely play key roles in his own decisions later in life for him as well, if he abandons his offspring or choses domineering partners in life. In the Black community and culture, the man has been replaced with Christ and a check, the Christ and a check often from the government via public assistance and religion, so consequently, we have generations of emasculated young Black men who are more comfortable with homosexuality and being feminine than masculine, as the masculine influence has been removed from his purview. Furthermore, it makes it look like Black women will lay with you but not stay with you.

Even the Bible states that woman was created for man, thereby ordaining the relationship and man's need for a woman and woman's need of a man. Black women between the ages of fifty and fifty-nine have been identified as the group most likely to get divorced. The study found that roughly half of white and Hispanic women in their early forties were stably married, compared to less than a third of Black women in the same age group.

Breaking things down further, under education is a systematic process whereas certain schools or schools zones are denied or don't receive the necessary funding from cities, counties, states, or the federal government, to ensure the educational needs of that segment of the community are being met. Now, if an individual is raised in an undereducated environment, they will likely academically struggle to keep up with their peers, rapidly falling behind, thereby having only two choices to either repeat the grade or drop out of school, which social pressure will likely encourage to them do the latter. Furthermore, standardized testing, said to be designed to ensure necessities are being taught, also serves as a systematic barrier to advancement thereby ensuring failure. In order to meet the standardized test matrix, many schools spend an inordinate amount of time teaching the standardized test, not educating the students. The results of the standardized test are then used for educational funding and the distribution of such resources, thereby placing the test and the outcomes high on the agenda of many educational administrations.

In the current the societal environment, an individual without an education is relegated to very few options for success, and these are criminality, entertainment, or entrepreneurship, all likely to fail without the right amount of talent, luck, and opportunity. There are plenty of talented and lucky people who will never have the opportunity to capitalize on their ability, which is a key factor of escaping their situation.

However, let's agree that a few will beat the odds and rise to prominence; what about the ones left behind? These are the ones that society will have to reckon with, the ones that will parent more disadvantaged children and will need social assistance with the children's cost of development and rearing. With an inadequate education and no options to obtain the necessities or niceties of life, often times procreation and criminality are the end results borne out of boredom and/or necessity, thereby adding more stress to a depressing situation. As disheartening as this sounds, people born into this environment will likely have negative encounters with law enforcement because police no longer regulate communities separating the good from the bad but are merely revenue stream creators eliciting opportunities for the city to generate income.

In today's environment, law enforcement's job is to find or suspect you of committing a violation and fine you (issue a citation), for which you will have to appear in court to answer to and as a minimum pay court cost. Municipalities have made the conscious decision to use the working poor and indigent as streams of revenue much like the ("pig and vagrancy laws of the past") via traffic fines, parking tickets, late fees, jaywalking citations, or the old stop-and-frisk, and hopefully find something because you look suspicious.

Moreover, with county jails and state prisons being administered by the for-profit private prison industry, coupled with an overburden criminal justice system, many municipalities are banking on the bondage.

A citizen being detained will create revenue for the municipality by the metropolis billing the federal government as the states and cities' cost of imprisonment is supplemented by the federal government. If an individual is convicted and given a mandatory minimum sentence, that is a guaranteed long-term source of federal funding. If you go to court and a judge agrees with your plight, you will still pay court cost and possible attorney fees if you don't have a public defender who would have likely plea bargained your case down to a fine and time severed or probation. You see, there is no way to escape without paying some sort of toll. If the judge disagrees with your plight, you will possible need the services of a bails bondsman to obtain your freedom, or you will remain in custody and probably lose your job or source of revenue.

Furthermore, institutionalized racism is promulgated through the established media outlets via highlighting the race of the perpetrator and the crimes committed by minorities at an increased and disproportionate rate than that of white criminals. No tribal demographic has cornered the market on crime; crimes are committed by all races, creeds, and colors, yet persons of African descent are overrepresented in the American penal system. Blacks make up 12 percent of the US population but 33 percent of the US prison population. When you are a member of a culture that has been a target of institutionalized racism for hundreds of years, you to tend to be more sensitive and aware of racial undertones and discrimination tactics. You become acutely aware of institutional efforts to paint your culture in a negative light. For example, programs such as surviving R. Kelly, and Leaving Neverland, and the prosecution and conviction of Bill Cosby makes you wonder, where are the programs on Working with Charlie Rose, Surviving the Catholic Clergy, Surviving Harvey Weinstein, Escaping Matt Lauer, or Trial and Conviction of Hugh Heffner? Why were these just as egregious actions downplayed, dismissed, or ignored, by the same media that persecuted the Black men in equal fashion?

Although slavery in America ended just over a 150 years ago, the descendants of those pioneers still suffer from the ideology that enslaved their forefathers. To be fair, some of the dogma is self-induced, and it is easier to blame others, and organizations, for the failures than accept the responsibility for their own inadequacies and actions, but nonetheless, there is justification for blame to be shared.

Education is the toll paid by the middle class to remain middle class and the fee paid by the poor to become middle class. In essence, it is the boarding pass to a better life, but ticket costs are high. In 2018 the average associate degree cost between twenty-five and thirty thousand dollars, a bachelor of science is forty-three thousand, and a graduate degree another forty thousand, with no guarantee of success; the minimum cost is $108,000; adding to that, if you need to borrow the money, a federal student loan will likely be the source. The current federal student loan base interest rate from Sallie Mae (the federal student loan monetary agency) is at 8 percent, leading one to ask, is it worth it? (Side note: federal student loan debt, much like delinquent federal taxes, is almost impossible to discharge in bankruptcy court like some other debt.) For many, the means doesn't outweigh the justification at the end. Why spend a $108,000 to get a fifty-thousand-a-year job, before taxes, all at a time when you are just starting out in life? Oddly enough, the interest rate on a federal home loan is 2.5 percent to 5 percent, so the question becomes, do they really want you to get the education, which you will need in order to afford a home? The end result is financial servitude, with no parole or time off for good behavior; you must pay your full debt to the system. In essence, student loans are a tax on the poor. Another option to escape, such as the one that I chose, requires you sign your life away to the military for an opportunity to get an education, which they will do their best distract you from by keeping you deployed, in professional development courses, job training, or by occupying your time with additional duties. The military's strength has always been at the expense of and on the backs of the poor and the lower middle class. Those willing to sacrifice their life for the opportunity to achieve a better existence, obtain an education or skillset, and advance with prestige beyond their peers. For the wealthy, national service is either family heritage or resume filler for their political aspirations, attempting to make themselves appear altruistic and or patriotic.

The military establishment true purpose is to be the enforcement arm of economic policy not the last resort if diplomacy fails as some may have you to believe. The Vietnam war was fought over President Lyndon Johnson's and his business constituents Southwest Asia oil investments, not the spread of Communism as history books would lead you to believe, just as the first Gulf war Operation Desert Shield was fought to retain access to cheap Kuwaiti, and Saudi Arabian oil and protect Western hemisphere countries corporate oil investments.

The Second Gulf War Operation, Enduring Freedom, was fought to take possession of Iraq's oil supply and remove Saddam Hussein from the top of Iraq's leadership chain as he had become defiant and combative to Western Hemisphere leadership's influence and demands. The official excuse given was we were fighting a war on terror against those who was threating our way of life. However, the fact of the matter is most terrorists and terrorism are borne out of poverty. What I've noticed is every country with high incidences of terrorism also has a large number of unemployed and unemployable disenfranchised fighting-age males with no direction and nothing to do. These groups of young men need a sense of purpose and directional bearing, and they often rally around a cause or the causes that blames others for their situations. Uniting around such viewpoints as the Western world has robbed them and other regions of the world of their natural resources, and this is why they don't or can't have a family of their own, i.e., Somalia's waters being overfished, Middle East robbed of its oil, and now we want Afghanistan's rare earth minerals.

In circumstances like Somalia, when the waters off their shores were overfished by Japanese and Western commercial fisheries, widespread famine ensued, and they turned to piracy to force compensation for the injustices bestowed upon them. Prior to the overfishing, Somalia was an unknown splotch land on Africa's coastline. Just as if it had not been for the discovery of oil in Saudi Arabia in 1938, Saudi Arabia would be an undeveloped African Sub-Saharan swath of land, but because of the oil, Saudi Arabia is one of the wealthiest countries on earth. To prove my point, every other Sub-Saharan country without oil falls well below the international poverty line, and a large majority of their citizens live in squalor. Financial bondage is the new indentured servitude, but this time they didn't just subjugate the Blacks but also the poor and middle classes, and any other minorities they could scoop up along the way.

Mass shooting and murders have become a common front-page story for American newspapers, and, sadly, more often throughout the world. Whether these massacres happen in Florida at a nightclub, Las Vegas at an outdoor concert, Texas at a Sunday morning church service, Denver, Colorado, at a movie theater, South Carolina in a church, Chicago at a parade, Washington State at a mall, or even Sandy Hook Elementary School in New

Town, Connecticut, the entire nation is covered, North, South, East, West, and Midwest, just to be sure. The point is, they, the government, wants your guns, specifically your assault rifles. You see, there is no valid reason anyone needs an assault rifle accept the military. You don't hunt with assault rifles, nor are they needed to protect your home, and we don't live in the Middle East or Africa, where the AK-47 is the weapon of choice to answer your door and greet your visitors. The fact is, assault rifles are only good for inflicting maximum damage in the minimum amount of time.

The NRA (National Rifle Association) has an extremely powerful lobbyist platform and they hide behind the Second Amendment of the US Constitution to push their agenda, the right to bear arms, and so far, the government has been powerless and unable or unwilling to get people to turn their weapons in. You see, what the government needs is for people to want to turn their rifles in and feel good about doing so for the greater good of society. The last thing the government needs is a public grassroots revolt over constitutional rights and the individual right to bear arms. There is an estimated three guns for every American man, woman, and child floating around the US, with more weapons being made daily. America is severely over-armed, Americans make up less than 5 percent of the world but owns 42 percent of the guns and we are loading up more every day. Besides, who is going to fight this war against American citizens for the government? The Army, Navy, Marines, Air Force, or perhaps the Space Force? Do you really expect the American military to turn on its mothers, fathers, brother, and sisters or children? No the government needs you to surrender without a fight.

Perhaps the unreasonable amount of guns on American inner-city and urban streets feed a larger agenda, possibly these guns are placed in the hands of the slow-witted and poor to facilitate organ harvesting? Maybe when we look at cities like Chicago, New York, Houston, or New Orleans, and many other large metropolises where murder runs rampant, guns are illegally and artificially pumped into these environments to facilitate murders so the victim's organs can be harvested to sustain the lives of rich and wealthy? You see, more organs are needed than donors are available, and with the possibility of rejection, the demand outweighs the supply; therefore, the supply must be increased by any means necessary. Most victims that die from inner-city gun violence will not get an independent autopsy; after all, why? The cause of death is evident, and the cost associated would be a waste of valuable resources.

So, with no pending autopsy looming, an organization would have free reign to access all the harvestable organs that were salvageable with no questions asked. The body would then be turned over to the funeral home to be embalmed, with the family and love ones never being the wiser. In July of 2013, a Georgia man was found dead in the Mojave Desert of California without any organs in his body. In October of the very same year, a Georgia teenager, whose body had been found rolled up in a wrestling mat, was buried without any of his internal organs as well and his body stuffed with newspaper. Additionally, in May of 2018, a fifteen-year-old Chicago teenage girl was found dead as well with her organs removed. It appears there evidently is a market and demand for viable organs, and at some level, people are willing to fulfill that demand by any means necessary.

For the longest we have spoken of and debated gun control, and after every mass shooting at a concert, mall, movie theater, church, school, parade, or senseless murder taking the lives of the innocent and unsuspecting, we unite and say something must be done. But what we have not done is address the root cause of the mass murders, which is the mental health crisis we now face and that we have been facing for decades.

A well-known fact is the mental health systems have always been poorly funded in the shadows of every financial plan of any state, federal, or municipal budgets. Nonetheless, the mental health care state of affairs was worsened when in the early nineteen eighties the then-President Ronald Regan defunded the federal portion concerning mental health, leaving it up to states to fund themselves. As irony is not without a sense of humor, John Hinckley, a man clearly with mental health issues, later endeavored to assassinate President Ronald Regan in an attempt to impress the actress Jodie Foster. As financial resources dwindled for mental health care, this coincidently was around the same time the homeless population started to precipitously grow, and that's because many of the homeless are mentally ill.

No sane individual choses to live in the elements and beg for sustenance not knowing if they will survive the night. So perhaps we don't have a gun control issue but a mental health crisis that's being masked by homelessness, and drug addiction, and ignored by the masses.

The system is broke, and we are overdue for a change, but change will not come until the comfortable become uncomfortable. You see, when the comfortable sees the less fortunate agonizing, it sparks empathy within them but not transformation; conversely, it is only when the situation affects the comfortable that change ensues shortly after. The change that I refer to is in the way we as a culture process the information we receive. We must make the information disseminators feel uncomfortable feeding us useless information to distract us from our enablable right to know, and decide our own fate as a nation.

History has repeatedly shown itself to be a liar when translated by those who seek to control the populace for their own selfish gains, and it is only through those who've questioned the irrational that the truth was finally revealed.

A revolution borne from mired reports of sexual assaults and inappropriate workplace relationships has taken society by storm with no industry left unscathed. From the president in the White House, and Congress alike, to the Supreme Court, the military, Hollywood, professional sports, the music industry, and the mass media itself, the victims are finding their voices and exalting a call for justice and equality. The assaulted, most of which were females, tell stories of extortion, humiliation, and belittlement, by the perpetrators in their selfish quest of sexual conquest, taking advantage of eagerness, aspiration for stardom, or desire for mentorship, and using the opportunity for an exercise in twisted self-gratification.

The revolt has adopted a take-no-prisoner approach, whereas the mere allegation of inappropriate behavior is cause for public condemnation and termination of the accused without any due process. Accusers and defendants alike both decry of the inequality and recount the event or events that led to this moment in time to the benefit of their current narrative.

Perception, sexism, entitlement, and relationship power all contribute to an environment ripe for corruption when the opportunity is presented.

Accusations ranging from decades old to months ago cast doubt if justice can ever be administered as time goes by. As I see it, if one person has dominion over another's career, income, or fate, a lack of true consent is inherently borne. Retribution is often hard to prove and almost never outrightly admitted by the perpetrators, whom often have the resources to tie the accusers and their accusations up in court so that righteousness becomes unaffordable. In many cases, the only justice available to the victims is karmatic (yes, I made this word up), by publicly smearing the names and reputations of the assailants, thereby bringing some sense of closure while simultaneously warning future victims.

It is not unreasonable to question history or what you've been told occurred in a particular sequence. In fact, you have a right, duty, and moral obligation to query events that you are told did not happen the ways you perceived them to have occurred but some other seemingly inexplicable manner which presents an alternative inconceivable by you at the time you witnessed it.

Once rulers of the nation, now tenants on reservations, the indigenous American people exist as a voiceless echoes from times past. Immigration is the new hotbed subject headlining newspapers from coast to coast, with talk of building walls and deporting people brought to the US illegally as children by their migrating parents seeking a better life. Immigration is used as a platform to run for public office, an excuse for crime increases, and a good place to hide racist views, but the truly interesting thing about immigration is it's the immigrants doing all the complaining. As I see it the Native Americans and Mexicans are the original settlers of this land, prior to the French, British, Portuguese, and Spaniards' arrival in the Americas and drawing lines in the sand, the indigenous people freely roamed the lands with no boarders to be respected.

It was only by the now-potentate's ancestors bringing diseases and overwhelming firepower was the Americas conquered, settled, and the land then divided into the different territories we have today. The French, British, Spanish, and Portuguese overwhelming desires to expand their national influences and hunger for gold was why the new world territories (the Americas) was explored, but even then they were too lazy to cultivate the land, so they imported immigrants and slaves to do the hard work of building a nation.

From the beginning of these notions, I didn't promise you you'd like, believe, or even agree with what you were about to read. Furthermore, I knew some of the hypotheses would be offensive and/or disturbing. My only assertion was they could shift your perception of reality, and I trust I delivered in that regard at least on some levels. Now you have a choice going forward to either question everything you think you know, or go on as a blind sheep being led to slaughter for your flesh and wool. The cover of this book was chosen because it embodies most of the content within. The color on the back cover was chosen as it represents your transition out of darkness into the enlightenment of knowledge. Going forward, before you pass judgement on me, I'll leave you with this one quote. James 1:19: "Be quick to listen, slow to speak, and slow to anger."

"Psychedelic Logic"
Drifts in the Perception of Reality
By
Barry F. Satchel

Knowledge is a funny thing; once you've been entrusted with it, you instantly have an obligation to do something with it. Whether you share it or keep it to yourself, you must make a decision. I recommend that you verify what you think you know to what you actually know, do the research, and discern the facts, but then what? It's not my intent to change the way you think but merely change the way you view the environment in which you operate. I'm not suggesting that you not trust anyone, but I am proposing that you trust your gut and not be so quick to believe what you hear from the various media outlets. It takes no effort to believe what you hear, a little effort to research what you've heard, and a lot of energy to react with the knowledge you've gained.